Emotional Turmoil

Courtney Einsig

BookLeaf Publishing

India | USA | UK

Presentation by *BookLeaf Publishing*

Web: www.bookleafpub.com

E-mail: info@bookleafpub.com

ISBN:9789358313635

First edition 2024

DEDICATION

Dedicated to those who made this possible; Evelyn, Molly, Kei, and to Ned who has supported me Unconditionally.

Crumbled Masks

Blood splatter and tear drops
Serrated knives and scars
Chalk lines on black tops
Suppressed feelings with SSRIs

Screaming, crying
Forced fake smiles
Everyone keeps lying
Hiding all emotions

Rainbows and sunshine
Laughter and love
All a facade to say "I'm fine"
Behind a worn out mask

As the mask starts to crumble
Let it fall to the floor
Your feelings begin to tumble
And your true self is exposed

Autumn

I aspire to be like Autumn.
Autumn embraces change;
cool weather, warm drinks, changing leaves,
shorter days, longer nights.

Autumn embraces change so gracefully,
even when it's falling to pieces;
flowers wilt, leaves fall.
Autumn makes change and falling to pieces a
work of art.

Autumn is a reminder that there is beauty
In letting go, changing directions, and
holding on to the last shimmer of hope and light
because it's never too late to start again.

Empty Smile

Seasons come and seasons go
Days go by and years go slow
Silent sounds fill the night
As darkened angel wings take flight

Corruption and regret fill the day
This pain can all be willed away
But these wounds won't seem to heal
No one understands the pain I feel

Whispered voices at my ear
Tell me things I don't want to hear
The truth drives me insane
My soul can't take this pain

It may heal, but will take a while
For now I'll continue with an empty smile

Love Is

Love is being confident in yourself and your
talents.
It's the smell of baking cookies and the feeling
of bliss.
Love is sunsets and the promise of a new day.
It's crazy dance moves in the middle of the
kitchen.

It's the constant nagging of parents
making sure you're okay.
It's being able to call or visit family
any time of the day and be greeted with open
arms.

Love is the support you surround yourself with
It's the friends you keep and who you love
Love is loving yourself, despite the flaws you
see
It's making plans and actually sticking to them.

Love is butterfly kisses, smiles, and laughter.
It's thunderstorms, lightning, and the smell of
rain.
Love is the little things that make every day
better
and the big things that make life worth living.

Dramatic Sarcastic Fantastic

They said grow up
Stop your cryin'
Put your chin up
And stop the whining

They couldn't see
who I could be
I'm just dramatic
A Lil bit sarcastic
All Around fantastic
You can't hurt me

Stand up straight
Hold your head high
Watch your weight
Don't forget to comply

They couldn't see
who I could be
I'm just dramatic
A Lil bit sarcastic
All Around fantastic
You can't hurt me

Bite your tongue
Grown ups are speaking

Aren't you a Lil young
To be critiquing

They couldn't see
who I could be
I'm just dramatic
A Lil bit sarcastic
All Around fantastic
You can't hurt me
So fuck you
And the expectation
I'm not here
for a confrontation
I'm just dramatic
A Lil bit sarcastic
All Around fantastic
You can't hurt me

Memories Flow

Minutes go.
Memories flow
My love for you will always grow.

Years go by
Time will fly.
My love for you will never die.

You're my night, you're my day.
You're the things I'll never say.
You're my shining light's ray.
When the world is dark and gray

You're the sun in the sky.
When the moon is far away
You're the fact within the lie.
When everything else has gone astray

My Love

My love for you is like a river,
Always flowing, never ending.
My love for you is like a rose,
Sweet and beautiful, always growing.
My love for you is like a rock,
Strong and steady, never budging.
My love for you is like a rainbow,
Always there during stormy skies.

Dreamland

In the light of night
Do you see for what you fight?
In the darkness of silence
Do you see the cause of violence?
In the loudness of whispers
Do you hear the words crisper?
The untold nightmares have begun.
For both the old and the young.
Dreamland stories are on the rise.
Of more dark and stormy skies.

The Time

In the darkness of shadows, here I stand
And to you I must command
For a job well done
That pleases none.

The ray of lights, my eyes do fight
For the time that we call night
When all goes right
And you use all your might.

The flickering stars they do call
For all of us near and far
The time has come, we must not fall
Instead we must risk it all.

The time is now
It has come
From the place we all are from
You can't ask how
You don't know why
You just keep going and giving it a try.

Childish Fears

Drowning in my own memories
Up to my neck in my childish fears
Thinking of you as I cry these tears
Wondering why you had to leave

Going through my past
Realizing it went by too fast
And that fate
Just didn't like me

Wondering when it's my time to shine
Wondering why you can't be mine
Then it's all clear
My dear
That it's just one of my childish fears

Visiting Angel

My tears fall down like rain
You, have none, you don't see what I do
My heart fills with sorrow knowing you'll be
leaving soon
You, stay the same, you don't know you'll be
leaving soon

For me time is going by so fast
For you, you live everyday as if none passed
There is so much for both of us to learn
But for you there is no way of teaching

You can't see how you're getting
I see it worsen when I visit
I remember the happy times
When I was little and you weren't sick
With a horrible
incurable disease
I hope you remember those times as well

You're my role model, the person I look up to
I just hope that when you do decide to leave
You'll think of me and the happy times
As an angel I hope that you will come to visit
me
Visit me in my dreams

Visit me in person just because
I just hope you're happy and pain-free
When you become a visiting angel

Love

You build me up
and bring me down
You make me happy
and make me sad
You are just hopes and dreams
yet you are the reason why I live
How can love be so strong
yet so weak

Season

The tree leaves fall
in the last autumn wind
As the first frost of winter
freezes everything over
The flowers grow back
as spring rolls in
The summer sun beats down
letting the world soak up its rays
Then the cycle starts again

Stars

As I lay here in my bed
I count the stars in the night
They are endless just like your eyes
It's a wonder they all fit in the skies
They dance through my dreams
As though it might seem
They are just glitter in the night

Speak Your Mind

Just speak your mind
And you will find
A whole new person
Down inside

Speak your voice
Voice your opinion
Don't hold back
They are not right or wrong

Speak your mind
And be heard
Voice your opinion
Be confident in your words

Waterfall of Life

Life is like a waterfall
Tranquil and peaceful
Until you reach crashing point
And problems start to form
You find yourself drowning
In your own thoughts
In other people's voices
That play nonstop
The crashing and beating
Hardly ever cease
When it does you're left
With a mess to fix
Until you're able to get out
And you encounter a fish or two
Small fixable problems
Until you come in contact
With another waterfall

Fake Flowers

When the flowers are fake
Can the love be real
Or does it all just fade away?
When the flowers are fake
Are they as beautiful
Or is there no beauty at all?
When the flowers are fake
Do they last as long
Or will they wilt twice as fast?
When the flowers are fake
Can the love be real?

Been there done that

Yeah, I've been there
Yeah, I've done that
I've had my world
Come crashing down on me
And in those moments
I was only there
No one else was to be found
I've seen heartbreak
Been thrust into madness
I've seen heartache
Turned to sadness
Been Isolated
And ignored
But I'm still standing
Nothing can knock me down anymore

Waterfall

21

The waterfall flows
Down the rocky water path
Watching time go by

Goodbye

Maybe I was stupid
For telling you goodbye
But you were the one
Who acted as if I didn't exist at times

Maybe I was stupid
For telling you goodbye
But maybe
We weren't supposed to be
In each other's lives

Maybe I was stupid
For telling you goodbye
But now I have to let you go
Hope for the best

Maybe I was stupid
For telling you goodbye
But maybe
We will make it into
Each other's lives again

But for now
This is goodbye

We are

We are like salt and pepper
We are like pencils and paper
We are like cats and dogs
Two opposites that go together

We are like black and white
We are like bacon and eggs
We are like day and night
Perfect opposites that attract

We are like sugar and spice
We are like apples and oranges
We are like yes and no
Two opposites that fit together

We are hot and cold
We are shy and bold
We are left and right
Perfect opposites that are balanced

We are two opposites
That go together
That attract
That stay with
each other
Forever

Storms

When the world has become a storm
You're the only one who can put it back into
verse form
With lulling words and serenades
The darkness just seems to fade
The day becomes clearer
And life is held more dearer
The thick fog that once clouded here
Has gone afar with a new fear
Its end is near
And calls for a cheer

Painted Dreams

Blank Canvas
Red, yellow, green, blue
Blank Slate
Grab a paintbrush old or new

Strokes here, strokes there
Add a splish or a splash
So many decisions could be made
Don't make them very rash

Bush, flower, sun, or stars
Add one or add them all
Insect, trees, animals or houses
Choose their size big or small

Hopes, dreams, love, trust
Add a sparkle of any one
Add your goals and yourself
Then you're done

These painted pictures
Are painted dreams
Uniquely yours
They make you shimmer, make you gleam

Drift Away

I close my eyes
I drift away
I make it through
My darkest days

I am falling
I rejoice
I am calling
Hear my voice

No one listens
Silence, screaming
No one cares
Thoughts, dreaming

I am pissed
And no one spares
Their time of day
A little breath

My Suicide

A quick slice
'Cross my wrist
Gonna let it cry
Its crimson tears
A quick pull
On the trigger
Gonna let it destroy
All of me
A rope here
Around my neck
Gonna let it rip
Through my skin
Which of these will be
My suicide

Scarlet Letters

These letters I write
Of my love for us
Is written in scarlet
The color of blood
Reminding me of
How much I long for you
And how you made me feel
But I know you won't get
These scarlet letters
For they are of when you
Once loved me
How could I have been so stupid
To have said yes when you asked
To go out with me
Now filled with regrets
My scarlet letters
Are now splashed
With the clear tears
That roll from my cheeks

Me

I'm not crazy
I'm just different
I'm not slow
I just go my own pace
I'm not short
I just need heels to make me tall
I'm not ugly
I just don't want to be pretty
I wear black
So I go unnoticed
I have answers for everything
Some just aren't that smart
I am me
And that's who I am
I don't need your approval
I'm not going to change

Remember When

Remember when I last saw you
You told me not to worry
You promised everything would be fine
Look where we are now
The promise you made was all a big lie
Remember when we laughed so hard
You told me I was crazy
You said that's why you loved me
You promised we would be the best of friends
Remember when the skies were gray
The rain fell pounding down on us
As we danced in circles
Look where that got us
Sick in bed
And remembering when

My Instant Death

Stab me in the chest
Not in the back
Create for me
My instant death
With piercing last breaths
And crimson blood drowning me
Do as you wish
But for me
Stab me in the chest
Not in the back
Create for me
My instant death

Fairy Tale

Fairy tales never come true
At least they don't for me
I don't have the fancy dress
I don't have the white horse
Or the royal parents
I'm not a princess
I don't have a prince
Why is it that only princesses
Can have the fairy tale endings
I feel as if I'm playing the villain
The villain whose story ends badly
Who doesn't have a redemption arc
Who's the outcast of the town
Why can't I play the princess for once
Why can't I have a fairy tale ending

Fear

Fear
It's what drives us
To cry our last tear
When we make a big fuss
Fear
Consumes us and scatters
All the things we hold dear
Everything that matters
Fear
Makes us lose
Makes us not want to see
All the roads we can choose
Fear
Has our imaginations on the run
Where reality is nowhere near
The damage is already done
Fear
Is our worst enemy
When we look into the past
When we look to what the future foresees

Red Rose

Your love is like sweet red roses
Each day I see it grows
Into something sweeter
With roots going deeper
My greatest wish is to see you smile
Even if it takes a while
Your kindness radiates in your heart
And that makes you a special work of art

My Dearest Love

My dearest love
I must admit
I cannot form words
For my love of you
My love goes deeper
Than the oceans
My love goes further
Than the stars
My dearest love
I must admit
My feelings for you
Will never end
The butterflies still tickle
Whenever you kiss me
My world still spins
When I see you smile
My dearest love
I must admit
I cannot form words
For my love of you
My dearest love
I must admit
My feelings for you
Will never end
My dearest love
I must admit

My love for you
Will never end

Sometimes

Sometimes I feel like crying
Laying down and maybe dying
But that's when I think of you
And how much I need you
How much you help me from myself

Sometimes I feel like crying
Laying down and maybe dying
But that's when I need you
To wrap your arms around me
To protect me from myself

Sometimes I feel like crying
Laying down and maybe dying
But that's when I want you
To say I'm always yours
To say I'm always needed here

Don't Exist

Can you hear me
Can you see me
I'm standing right here
Yelling until my voice goes numb
But you don't listen
As if I don't exist

Can you hear me
Can you see me
I'm standing right here
Calling out for someone to save me
But you look past me
As if I don't exist

Can you hear me
Can you see me
I'm standing right here
Drowning in the tears I cry
But you don't care
Because I don't exist

Strong

Can you stay strong
Strong enough for me
To fight off what I can't
Am I strong enough
To fight away all the shadows
That are consuming me
That are taking away all the light
Will I be strong enough
To cast away my fears
To finally be free
From the shadowy fate of mine
Can I be strong enough
To always be happy
To never let the mask fall
To conquer the shadows

Blue and White Madness

The school bell rings again
Children file out of the
Old ivy infested building
All dressed in blue and white
Little do they realize
The tree branches reaching out
And the shadows lurking in every corner
As they leave holding hands
With their moms and dads
All except one little girl
Sitting on the swing
With the wind whispering to her
And rocking the creaking swing
She's all alone with no one there to hold her
hand
With tears in her eyes
She willingly walks towards the shadows
Slowly driving herself into madness

Sea Turtle

The sea turtle swims
Gracefully in the open
Looking for a friend

Time

Time floats along the surface
Invisible but still lurking there
Slowly dragging days along

Misunderstood

You call me smart
You like my art
But yet you cannot see
Who I'm supposed to be
My friends all know
All of my foes
They see me
How I'm supposed to be
Why can't you be more like them

Yin and Yang

Day and night
Black and white
Can't you see we're just too different
Sun and rain
Comfort and pain
Can't you see we can't get along
Hot and cold
Shy and bold
Can't you see it just won't work
Good and bad
Happy and sad
It just won't work
Can't you see we can't get along
Can't you see we're just too different
Me and You

Aunt Coco's House

45

At Aunt Coco's house
There's laughter and smiles
It's never as quiet as a mouse
There's a mountain of dishes
And loads of laundry to do
But there's always time
For hugs and kisses
There's food in the cabinets
And an open door
There's a warm home
Waiting to greet you with arms wide open
At Aunt Coco's house
There's arts and crafts
Paint and glitter all over the floors
There's floors to be mopped
And windows with fingerprints
But there's always time
For playing and cuddles
There's blankets for forts
And songs to sing
Dances to dance
And fun to be had

Winter

I want to dance like Winter.
Winter dances on the line of beauty and chaos;
Cold air, snow days, hot cocoa
Picture perfect scenery, magic
Winter embraces the beauty and chaos
Even when people despise it;
Accidents, delays, power outages.
Yet, Winter isn't phased by anything.
Winter is a reminder that there is beauty within
the chaos, to dance like no one is watching, and
to keep the magic alive that you felt as a child.
Because the only validation you need is
yourself.